CATHURES

EDWIN MORGAN was born in Glasgow in 1920. He became lecturer in English at the University of Glasgow, from which he retired as titular Professor in 1980. He was appointed Poet Laureate of Glasgow in 1999, and received the Queen's Gold Medal for Poetry in 2000.

EDWIN MORGAN

Cathures

New Poems 1997–2001

CARCANET Mariscat

Acknowledgements

Thanks are due to the editors of the following publications in which poems first appeared: *Around the Globe, Back to the Light* (Mariscat/Glasgow City Council), *Borderline* (Mainstream), *Cencrastus, Chapman, Cutting Teeth, The Dark Horse, The Drouth, Earth Love, The Herald, London Review of Books, New Shetlander, New Writing 8, New Writing 9* (Vintage), *News for the Ear, Nomad, Poetry Ireland, Poetry Review, Painted, Spoken, Scotland on Sunday, The Scotsman, Such Strange Joy: Ten Years of Shore Poets* (iynx), *Sunday Herald, Times Literary Supplement, Understanding, Unknown Is Best* (Mariscat/Scottish Poetry Library).

First published in 2002 by
Carcanet Press Limited
4th Floor, Alliance House
28-34 Cross Street
Manchester M2 7AQ
&
Mariscat Press
3 Mariscat Road
Glasgow G41 4ND
mariscatpress@hotmail.com

A CIP catalogue record for this book
is available from the British Library

ISBN 1 85754 617 2

The publisher acknowledges financial assistance
from the Arts Council of England

Set in Times Roman by XL Publishing Services, Tiverton
Printed and bound in England by SRP Ltd, Exeter

'...as far as Cathures, which is now called Glascu'

– Jocelin of Furness, *Life of Kentigern*

Note

Demon was published in a small edition by Mariscat Press in 1999. *The Trondheim Requiem* was commissioned by the composer Ståle Kleinberg for performance in Trondheim Cathedral in 2002. 'On the Bus' was commissioned by BBC Radio 4 for National Poetry Day 2001. 'Robert Burns', 'Burke and Hare', 'Janet Horne', 'Madeleine Smith', 'John Muir' and 'Helen Adam' were commissioned in 2000 by Glasgow International Jazz Festival and set to music by Tommy Smith as part of *Sons and Daughters of Alba*. 'Galoshin', 'Blind', 'Gallus', 'Leonids', 'Junkie' and 'Sunset' were written for an Easter 2000 programme on BBC2.

Glasgow City Council appointed me Poet Laureate of the city in 1999, and many Glasgow poems in the book were stimulated by that appointment. Equally, there are many poems outwith this connection, since (as Lucretius pointed out) it does not matter in what part of the universe you live:

> Nec refert quibus adsistas regionibus eius:
> usque adeo, quem quisque locus possedit, in omnis
> tantundem partis infinitum omne relinquit.

E.M.

Contents

NINE IN GLASGOW

Pelagius

I, Morgan, whom the Romans call Pelagius,
Am back in my own place, my green Cathures
By the frisky firth of salmon, by the open sea
Not far, place of my name, at the end of things
As it must seem. But it is not a dream
Those voyages, my hair grew white at the tiller,
I have been where I say I have been,
And my cheek still burns for the world.
That sarcophagus by the Molendinar –
Keep the lid on, I am not stepping into it yet!
I used to think of the grey rain and the clouds
From my hot cave in the Negev, I shooed
The scuttle of scorpions. I had a hat –
You should have seen me – against the sun
At its zenith in that angry Palestine.
I spoke; I had crowds; there was a demon in me.
There had been crowds four centuries before,
And what had come of that? That was the question.
I did not keep back what I had to say.
Some were alarmed. They did not like my red hair.
But I had a corps of friends who shouldered
Every disfavour aside, took ship with me
Westward over the heaving central sea.
We came to Carthage then, and not alone.
The city was seething livid with refugees.
Such scenes, such languages! Such language!
The Goths were in Rome. I saw a master
I had studied under, wild-eyed,
Clutching tattered scrolls, running.
I saw a drift of actors with baskets
Brimming broken masks, they gestured
Bewildered beyond any mime.
I saw a gladiator with half a sword.
I heard a Berber's fiddle twang like the end of a world.
Morgan, I said to myself, take note,
Take heart. In a time of confusion

You must make a stand. There is a chrysalis
Throbbing to disgorge oppression and pessimism,
Proscription, prescription, conscription,
Praying mantises. Cut them down!

One stood against me:
Distinguished turncoat, ex-Manichee, ex this and that,
Preacher of chastity with a son in tow,
A Christian pistoned by new-found fervour,
Born of the desert sand in occupied land,
Born my exact coeval but not my coadjutor,
Bishop in Hippo brandishing anathemas,
Bristling with intelligence not my intelligence,
Black-hearted but indefatigable –
Augustine! You know who you are
And I know who you are and we shall die
Coeval as we came to life coeval.
We are old. The dark is not far off.
It is four hundred years now since those nails
Were hammered in that split the world
And not just flesh. Text and anti-text
Crush the light. You can win,
Will win, I can see that, crowd me out
With power of councils, but me –
Do you know me, can you believe
I have something you cannot have –
My city, not the city of God –
It is to come, and why, do you know why?

Because no one will believe without a splash from a font
Their baby will howl in eternal cold, or fire,
And no one will suffer the elect without merit
To lord it over a cringing flock, and no one
Is doomed by Adam's sin to sin for ever,
And who says Adam's action was a sin,
Or Eve's, when they let history in.

Sometimes when I stand on Blythswood Hill
And strain my eyes (they are old now) to catch
Those changing lights of evening, and the clouds
Going their fiery way towards the firth,
I think we must just be ourselves at last
And wait like prophets – no, not wait, work! –
As prophets do, to see the props dissolve,
The crutches, threats, vain promises,
Altars, ordinances, comminations
Melt off into forgetfulness.
My robe flaps; a gull swoops; man is all.
Cathurian towers will ring this hill.
Engines unheard of yet will walk the Clyde.
I do not even need to raise my arms,
My blessing breathes with the earth.
It is for the unborn, to accomplish their will
With amazing, but only human, grace.

Merlin

What time, what year, what universe, all's one.
I have been seen in crowded courts and in fields
And by long roads and on great waters.
No one knows where to have me, but
Who is there who does not know of me?
I made some rough magic for King Roderick.
He fed me in his court on Dumbarton Rock.
He pleased me in his palace at Partick.
He took me to talk to his countryman
Kentigern whom I took to as well as talked to
As we bantered over a beaker the difference
Between the miraculous and the maroculous.
Good days those, out of many not good!
Men went to war; Roderick went; I went.
I am no fighter, why should I go?
'Record my victory,' said Roderick.
'You are a bard. Sing me.' Sing what?

The victory of death, the cries, the rolling limbs,
Clang of swords and reddening of grass,
The pain that rises to the grand indifference
Of clouds as they muffle past, the fury
That hunts the pain that hunts the clouds –
All that, but then I watched the head of a friend
Bounce down the hill, blood path, not bearable.

Battles end, and surgeons come, and ravens.
A horn blew truce, but nothing could console me.
Was I to sing that a king had won?
War wins wounds, widows, it eclipses the sun
For many. I could only run,
I wailed, roared, tore my tunic, tore myself
From every restraining hand, took to the wilds,
Half mad, or mad indeed as some men said,
Tunnelling into the Caledonian forest.

How long did I live there? What is time?
I became a green man, man of the woods,
My beard grew, I ate roots and nuts,
I had mulberries and rain for my dinner.
Only the wolf, grey wolf, dear wolf
Was mine to roam the thickets with.
Best of companions, better than man,
You followed me who had nothing to give,
Your hair was white with age, you limped,
You stretched beside me, howling faintly
Under the cold leaves and the constellations.

Those who found me came softly, playing lutes.
They put my wasted body on a litter,
Carried me back into humanity.
I held the burning eyes of the wolf
Till the very last moment. The madness was gone,
And now I must make the most of men.

I am living here in my house of glass
On Cathkin Hill, above the twinkling lights
Of Cathures with its sweet green hollows.
It is not glass, not smoke, not even air
But has its own dimension. My sister Gwen
Helps me in my observatory.
I am told she is like Ada, Byron's daughter,
Mathematician before her time.
With our double vision we untwist binary stars.
A light kiss then, and do we have phantom supper?
Do you think we would tell you! Naw naw,
As they say in Cathures. We donate our spirit
To that gallus city. We are quicksilver
With no mould to run into. Watch us change.
This glass house which is not made of glass
Is Merlin's esplumoir, his moulting-cage
Where high above the rambling Molendinar
He waits until the new enchanter
Flashes a more formidable feather
And that, too, not for ever.

Thennoch

Crowns and carpets – I might have been a queen.
But bowing and scraping was never my style.
The king my father – and it hardly grieves me to say so –
King Loth was a tyrant of the old school.
Daughters were sent for dynastic soldering.
Lothian was out on a limb – what to do?
I was given – given like a shiny parcel
To a Cumbrian prince, a boor and a slobberer
But devious with it – my veils and bells
Would be finest and loudest, my dowry dizziest –
No thanks, no thanks at all, no, not at all!
The fells and ghylls can keep Prince Ewen!
– Well, that made it apoplexy time.
Loth was like Lear a thousand years ago.
I was banished to feed pigs on the heath.
My randy weirdo suitor was dead bent –
Bent, that's the word, dear god – on having me,
Put on skirt and kerchief and high voice
For friendly chat in the fields, but then
Jumped me like Dracula, humped me, dumped me
Bleeding into the innocent soil.

Rebellion was bad; pregnancy worse.
They threw me down a hill to kill
Me and the new life both. No, I said no,
No thank you, no, not at all. I rolled
Like a ball, hugging and cradling the seed.
I was not broken, I said I was not broken!
So they sent me to sea in an old battered boat
With no oars or rudder, my hands bound behind me:
That should do the trick. As you see, it did not.
I was driven ashore at happy Culross
Where I was cared for, and my son was born.

How far it seems from Culross to Cathures
With its ships and its crowds and its many tongues!
But its folk were good to the lass from Fife.
I have lived here now to a strong old age.
'Women,' I tell my maids – I have just three –
Nothing ostentatious or stiff – 'Women,
You must be strong. Speak your mind. Exist.
Don't curtsey to me because my son is a bishop.'
They take it all in, polishing the pewter
As if it offended them. They have an edge,
A raucous life which I well know about.
No swearing in the parlour though: fair's fair.
My son does well; we are still close;
The people show their affection, call him Mungo.
He may not be holier-than-thou – I hope not –
But he is certainly holier than me!
No doubt we have to put up with choirs,
With processions, with vestments, with candles –
What a drip and stink, must be cheap tallow –
With words intoned and knees on stone and
Oh I don't know what what what –
What makes a pagan sing,
A bird, a whetstone, even
The stars, as scholars say –
I keep these thoughts, and do my work, and sing.

I love to clamber up to Gilmore Hill –
My joints complain, but I can do it –
On one of those fine still forenoons
When summer mists have only just dispersed
To show the winding glint of Kelvin water
Going its way among the greenery,
The green ravine, the dearest green.
Although I cannot see it from that hill,
I know there is a green glade in the city,
A square glade where a single ancient tree
Overshadows a well, a well of the clearest
Where many cups have been filled. My cup
Would be filled to overflowing
To be buried there in that quiet place
In the midst of the coming and going.

George Fox

All right, it was time to be a pilgrim.
Dreary Middle England I got through,
Rode a poor horse and sold it, bought a better,
Steaming and shivering under the wild trees
In drasty weather, devilish wet,
Handful of oats, knuckle of cheese,
Waiting for gale to dwindle to breeze,
Praying a bit but only a bit,
Gerrup, Silver! and George get off your knees!
It's no more than another moor or two,
How many lines of thorny wind-bent hedge –
And please, no foxy metaphors about thorns,
We're pilgrims all, sure, no sweat, no crowns,
It presses on my temples without blood,
The earth, the folk who cry or do not cry –
Where was I? oh yes, going north,
It's only miles, curlews, lead-mines, ruins,
Sheep in the crumbling keep, rabbits asleep –
Until I followed the dull shine
Of the Clyde rolling fish-full and dark
Towards the towers of that dark
Place, that Glasgow, where I must fish
For souls, oh, splash them into light.

I have preached the word, and a good word it is,
In fields and market-squares and meeting-houses.
Sometimes sullen faces glum up at me,
Or sceptic sneers lurking on the sidelines.
What in God's name (God forgive me!) is wrong
With the people of Glasgow who have not even the wit
To be sullen, far less the chutzpah to sneer?
Admittedly I arrived somewhat dusty
At one of the city gates, I was not dapper,
Uncouth was the word no doubt,
Suspicious the alien vocables of Leicestershire!
The grim guard took me to the magistrate.
I kept my hat on as I always do.
Men of authority are men of straw.
I was polite and he was polite.

Perhaps he thought me mad, but harmless.
I was at liberty, he said, to hold a meeting
In the town centre, open to all.
Well, I have had meetings and meetings,
A hundred folk, a dozen, even five,
But never till now have I had none.
Not one, no, not a single soul,
Not a child, not even a dog
Came to listen to the best of news
They would ever hear in this life,
In this city, in this vale of darkness.

Were they all too busy making money?
Were they stuffing their stores with calico and claret?
Were they bent over balances, or boosting their buildings?
Were they bolting salmon and slapping their bellies?
Were they raging and searching for runaway slaves?
Their trades and their trons and their trappings are trash.
Is it gold you want to stash?
All that brilliant bullion?
Bullion is ash!

I could deliver nothing in that place.
I was shot of Glasgow, I came away.
I say I was shot of that Glasgow!
Pedlar Satan can pad up and open his case.

John Hunter

My dear young man, you must learn to be quick.
If I go off at a tangent, you must follow.
My mind is not a standing loch, it churns,
It throws up roots and vestiges of things
In clutter, tangle, lawlessness –
Or is it cluster, triangle, logarithms?
As I was saying before you raised your eyebrows,
I macerated the Irish giant in my boiler –
You know the copper boiler, would boil a whale
The apprentice said, which was not so daft
As not to give me an idea, but anyhow –
The skeleton would grace my medical school
For both art and instruction, lording it a little
Over albino mavises and fossils –
Don't forget, though, I need fossils,
Medicine can learn from the rocks,
It's not all blawflum, there's a story,
Ammonites will do, keep your eye open –
If you think I am a collector, you are right –
And so is my brother William, there's no shame
In a Hunterian Pandora's box, it will go
To Glasgow, to that University
Where William studied theology five years,
Came out sane and did obstetrics, what a man –
Anyhow, I am glad you have kept in touch,
Your dogfish arrived in reasonable condition
(My wife nipped her nose, but she understands),
A large porpoise would go down very well now
If you still have sea friends, and oh yes
What the devil becomes of eels in winter,
I don't want eels, I want information,
If you know any skippers , trawlermen –
What's that? – yes yes, you have things to do,
But just if you can, if you can – the mind
Can be stretched like cahootchy, it's magic
If you want it to be – don't frown, man! –
It isn't every day you get someone like me
To unsettle you. – Congratulations, by the by,
I hear you got married, she has money too? –

Well, all the better! – But remember our cuckoos:
I want to know far more than I know:
Shoot an old one, send me its gizzard in spirits.
– It is getting dark. Let's light a lamp.

A good time this twilight, when the bats come out.
If you catch any, let me have some.
I need to count their pulse, their breath.
And do you know I am hedgehogless?
You sent me two for my garden –
One an eagle ate, a ferret the other –
More please! You see how greedy I am!
And now I am into vegetables:
Would you guess that the energy of a vine –
Think of it pulsing away, sap for blood –
Can raise a column of fluid five times higher
Than a horse can do it – green muscles eh?
Is it one world? Of course it is!
Think crystals. Regular? Dead?
But some are irregular as trees.
Deviation is as good as law.
No wonder William dropped divinity!
I see you are not shocked: good man.
Someday I shall be quite famous.
Someday my brother will be famous.
Someday, young Jenner, you will be famous too.
Don't bridle, it is my prophecy. Guaranteed.

Dark now, dark thoughts, battlefield-dark.
I was an army surgeon in the field.
The flares and flashes, smoke and crack and shriek,
Long agonies for some, dismemberment,
Waiting for anything science could do
To stop the pain, the pain – to have been there,
And kept the head, and helped, and stanched and patched,
Brought me where medicine pours into reality
Its desperately hopeful salve.
I specialized in gunshot wounds.
I made some finds.
I went my rounds
As you must do, young man, with patience
For enemies and for friends.

Vincent Lunardi

I do not know what is wrong with me.
I am sick, I lie like lead on this bed.
The sisters took me in. I hear their bells
And the dull rumour of Lisbon beyond these walls.
I am so poor I have nothing.
I have nothing and I am nothing.
The world has shrunk to a bowl of gruel
When the sun goes down. Another world
Is not yet closed, my memories.
I summon them and they come running.
Why can I not rise to greet them?
To rise was my life, I was born for it!

I still remember that early dream of flight.
Playing in the olive groves of Lucca
I stretched my arms to match the dragonflies,
Buzzed and zigzagged like a bee, but most,
Oh most and best, I watched the summer swallow
Slicing the air with a rapture I gave to it
From my own longing. I would have the air,
I would have it someday!
                         Twenty years ago
The air was indeed mine, I was an aeronaut –
I was not the first, I don't claim that, but
I was noted, I was marked, I was famous,
I was loved, I was honoured, I was fêted
In England and Scotland, Italy and Spain,
Even in dusty Portugal where I am dying.
But I am not talking about death!
I am talking about life and life abundant!
I have enough breath to spell it.
Memory breaks the sound barrier.
We are off and away, back to happy Glasgow
Where I rose twice from the dead
Tussocks of Glasgow Green and made a wonder.
The hydrogen roared, the flaccid silk blossomed
To a great pod of pink and yellow and green
Stretched taut and shimmering into the blue.
I leapt into the decorated basket,

Decorative myself if I may say so,
Dressed in my regimental colours –
Neapolitan if you want to know –
With a good leg, many ladies commend it,
Waving my flag and blowing my speaking-trumpet
While a band blared the most rousing of marches,
Bells were pealed, and the people waved
To my waving, and exclaimed and shouted and whistled
From tens of thousands of upturned faces
As my six-men-high balloon majestically
Lifted above that ever-living city.
Do you think I cut a figure, cut a dash
In that airy cabin, in my stockings of silk,
My lacy cuffs, my goffered cravat, my – ah,
That hat! – was I not gay that day
And was it not the gayest of days?
The ladies thought so: some clapped, some fainted,
All had eyes for the aeronaut. Do you know
Some of them later helped me to patch
A rent in the balloon, and I gave them
A thread or two of silk: some said
It would become a locket in their bosoms.
Why do I say these things? I had no lady.
I danced a minuet, kissed here and there.
But my only bride was the high air.

I wonder who will remember Lunardi
That soared among the clouds and saw below him
Trongate and Tontine, and the Saracen's Head
Where he lodged and talked the night into pleasure?
It is like a dream of the gay times
That are possible and to be so cherished
We have a little comfort to be taken
As the shadows close in. They do, they do.
It is cold too. Who is that standing in the door?

John Tennant

Tennant's Stalk – that's my monument.
Talk of the town, top of the walk, tells them to stop,
Any that trudge by that well-named Sight Hill.
It tapers elegant to its hourly bloom,
Thick smoke, acrid, highest anywhere,
Four hundred and thirty blessed feet
Above my empire, my chemical empire,
My blessed St Rollox, biggest anywhere,
My eighty acres of evenhandedly
Distributing industry and desolation!
Chief of all chimneys, carry your noxiousness
Into the clouds and away from my employees,
Settling if it must where I cannot see it!
I am in business for the uses of the world,
Bleaching powder, soap, sulphuric acid,
A thousand casks a week from my cooperage.
I'm standing here in the midst of furnaces
Which I understand and command – oh yes,
If there is anything new or strange in chemistry
It will not be the case that I have not heard of it.

Boasting, in my Glasgow way? Well, perhaps.
I am a chemist with passions. I am a character,
They say. Take my wife. I don't mean take my wife,
But just consider. We are not married
Except by good old Scottish cohabitation.
She is a total non-person to my family.
My brother, well we don't get on, that's that.
My sister-in-law, put bluntly, is a bitch.
My dear Rosina was a factory girl,
She may be beautiful, she may be bright –
She *is* beautiful, she *is* bright –
But a lassie from St Rollox, that's not on.
Well well, I've put their gas in a peep,
That claque or clat of bitches who can't stand
Class mix – my grand house in West George Street
Has, or should I say boasts, a fine brass plate
For MR & MRS JOHN TENNANT. And that's us.

How can a rebel be a capitalist?
What's the problem? I have a yacht – of *course*! –
And some have tried to poach my butler – fat chance –
But who was it marched through Glasgow in '32
To see the great Reform Bill safely through?
Who was it planted a doctor in the works
To give free treatment to all? Who ran
A factory school for workers' weans? Who
Cranked up mechanics' institutes? Who stayed
In the centre of Glasgow when the nabobs and nobs
Hustled out to suburban palazzos?
I'm bluff and gruff and tough enough,
If a foreman is a pain in the arse
I tell him he's a pain in the arse.
My eyebrows are bushy, and if my finger is in my fob
You had better watch out if you are skiving your job.
But, or rather BUT,
If ever you are down on your luck
You can come to me, you can run
With a secret misery, I can cut
Corners for you, nothing is shut
That John Tennant cannot get unstuck.

I come back to my Stalk, my obelisk, my watchtower,
My beautiful slender avant-garde polluter.
What poet would sing those acres of grey ash,
That ghastly guff of hydrogen sulphide?
Who cares? I'm happy to stand in for Homer.
His gods would have cackled with joy
To see my new-born boy
Poking manfully towards their heavenly rookery.
I marked the occasion – oh, did I not!
I gathered a posse of friends to hansel the Stalk.
Ladies and gents, I said, you're going to the top!
Such cries of horror, it was like a play.
I relished the moment, lifted a hand
For the clamour to subside. Just a joke, folks.
I don't need steeplejacks. It's *inside* you're going.
The bricks are the best money can buy,
They are new, they are brilliant, not a smitch of soot.
Please admire them as you rise past them.

Climb? Not a step. You will mount like magic
By a system of hissing steam-powered pulleys –
O James blessed Watt, late of this parish! –
Emerge at the viewing platform, safe as houses,
And sweep your eyes around like modern gods.
What's that sir? Insurance? Christ man
This is Glasgow. You are pioneers. Get in.
There's a woman in the Stalk before you.
Yes ma'am? Skirts? That's taken care of.
No one will look up your furbelows.
The ladies will sit in a basket, like balloonists.
The gents will be in buckets, like Brahmins.

Well, up they went into the half dark,
Clutching their ropes, listening to the pulley,
Silenced by the mystery.
The summit was all light and air and chatter.
The smoky city was shunting fiercely below
But the height, the horizon, the haze was their hope
As they looked at, looked for, Scotland.
The firth, the masts and sails, the Arran hills,
The river winding south through glasshouses,
Eastward a faint glint of spires – Edinburgh?
We don't want Edinburgh! Find Ben Lomond!
They found it, and they found much else
As they leaned on my parapet, not paradise
But a throb of the great paradox,
Useful filth, mitigated pain,
Crops of brick and iron, with or without rain.

Louis Kossuth

This is not the Great Hungarian Plain
But I can be almost content here in Turin
Watching the sparrows at their dust-baths and the sun
Splashing new factories with bright hard light –
It goes, this place, it hums, it buzzes, capital
Of Italy's long-sought unity, ex-French
As Hungary is oh, not yet, ex-Austrian!
The Danube can only flow through my dreams.
It feeds a forest of forty years exile
In my nightmares. My dreams are nightmares.

Wake up! the bell says as the pigeons scatter.
Coffee (not as good as Turkish, but still –)
And I am writing in a book, at my window.
What I record is at least mine,
A man of this time,
I lay it on the line.
The lost republic had a president
In its brief life; I was that president
Till Slav and Teuton squeezed that brief life out
And I was squeezed even of my citizenship
Of the land I was born to, an exile, a wanderer.
Turks were good to me, Americans, English,
Scots, and now Italians, but longings
Are inextinguishable, exact, and sad.

Who does not know Hungary? I spoke
To many thousands, pleading for hope.
I worried them like a dog with a bone.
My black beard grew grey as some seeds were sown
For Magyar soul and Magyar home.
But for all my denouncing of empire and throne
The emperor still sits on his throne.

What kept me going? Oh there were times,
Meetings that crackled like an open fire.
Glasgow was extraordinary, unforgettable.
Evening in Argyle Street, what a crush, what a mix –
Drunks and dandies, ladies swishing silks,

Such swearing, such spitting, such singing,
Such clouds of tobacco, such scents of Havana,
Such pushing to the wall, such grins and galoshes –
And once I got to the City Hall
Such a press of police expertly manhandling
A yell of youths and girls at the entrance
Eager to emulate the revolutionaries
Of '48, not so long ago – but inside
I mounted the platform before three thousand
Faces raised in patient expectation.
They were with me all the way; my tale
Was of freedom and oppression, the hopes of men.
For my small country, as for theirs,
The right to look after our own affairs,
Not louting low to the big battalions,
Must be and would be paramount.
Liberty is golden and eternal.
Would you see your children in chains?
– And then I crowned my peroration
By beckoning forward my two young sons,
Goodlooking teenagers, who took a deep bow.
The audience went wild, cheering, clapping,
Standing, shouting, some of them in tears,
Shaking my hand as we left the hall.

Was it theatre? Some say I am a showman.
Well, there was theatre to come, oh yes.
I was buttonholed by a skelf of a man,
Smelling of whisky but lucid, intense,
Poet of sorts, clutching manuscripts.
I always speak to people, which in Glasgow
Is acceptable. His name was Macfarlan.
Did he like my speech, I asked him.
He said What is the use of independence
If you are living on potatoes and black bread?
I said What is the use of caviar
If it comes to you on a colonial plate?
He said All I want is three meals a day
Under a roof that won't let in the rain.
I said That's the sort of thing that pleases
Tyrants: keep the people cowed and sweet.

He said England is not exactly a tyrant.
I said Maybe not, but think about it.
Until the word Austro-Hungarian is obsolete
I shall never return to Budapest.
I am not touring Europe for social conditions.
He said Maybe you should be. I said Maybe,
But I'm not. I want my country first,
Then all the social changes that it needs.
I've seen the tombs of Washington and Burns.
He frowned, gave me a pamphlet, hurried off.

I close my book and put away my pen.
Memory has flooded every creek and crack
Till I sit back and let myself be carried
Into a dark so far that at the last
I hardly hear the storm outside
Coming to test my shaking glass,
The shutter and its hasp.
But I do hear it, rise, and make all fast.

Enrico Cocozza

Enrico, Rico, Coco, call me what you will,
A Glasgow man always responds.
If I like you, and have use for you,
I shall invite you to join my circle
Behind the café. It's just films, films.
I am always looking for new talent.
My passion is the whirr of the camera.
I point it in ways unwhirred before,
At least in these benighted parts. See film?
Immediate: bare: the image: no escape.
Clodhopping storytelling bites the dust.
This is the century of *this*, not that.

Documentary? I've done slums and docks,
But there's another world, out there, in here.
Sure, Grierson was worthy, Grierson was great,
Scottish hero, put it on the screen,
Scotland, no Brigadoon, aye aye, right.
Drifters was shown to the Herring Board:
Even the herring were bored. Sorry, John!
See worthiness? That is Scotland's shame.
One thing you can say about Glasgow,
It is not worthy, and neither am I.
Rico has other fish to fly.
Glasgow is Gotham City. Porphyria's lover
Has wound her strangling hair about her throat
Many times, and Browning has not said a word.
Dark times, I've seen her, she is worth a shot.
Grainy murders, brooding suicides –
Sinister is as sinister does? –
It is only a movie, my dear.
True, I keep my tombstone in my room,
But that's a movie too. You have to live it
If you want to shoot it. Bygod you have to live it.

Problems? You name it, I have them.
But you will not find me bent over a tear-bottle.
I am hardly alone. Did he not have problems,
That master of my craft, that Eisenstein?
He knew he was *one of those*. He was ashamed of it,
Afraid of it, it was all pathology, pathetic.
He cruised the Berlin clubs in iron trousers.
He scanned his Freud and found a purple sublime
In the silky sublimations of cinematography.
Celluloid sailors wouldn't beat you up!
Censors would frown, but what did they know?
'My lips have only touched the cup of life.'
That's what he wrote, but it's not really so.
I love the way he scoured the crowds and pounced
On a startled hotel boilerman to act
His vision of the foxy-eyed ship's surgeon
Peering through that pince-nez in *Potemkin*.
These transformations were a second life
To him: greasy cap to officer's cap,
Imagination straddling the class gap.

I like to feel it warm between my knees –
No no, not that! – my pair of bongo drums.
You can see me at it in my own film
Bongo Erotico, quite gallus, banging it out,
Sporting some very sultry eyeshadow,
Smoking a stubby sultry cigarillo,
Staring sultrily at my favourite dancer
As he sways in his sloppy satin knickers.
Well it's not *Braveheart*, and it's not *Little Women*,
But what it is it is, some flesh and heat
Flushed out of Fifties forbiddenness.
Oh there were so many hidden souls
Searching for what in this life could not be found!
The picture-palaces were glittering –
Green's Playho se ('We want "u" in'),
Grand Central, Classic, Curzon –
Glittering but filled with shadows,
Community of shadows on the screen,
Community of shadows in the stalls,
Great coming and going – Patrons Who Persist

In Changing Their Seats Will be Ejected –
Silent surge like the one Dante observed
As it *andava continuamente*
Over the sandy plain.
Whatever the shame, whatever the stain,
Dante would sigh to see
Those lost ones sitting in the smoky dark
With their *mal protesi nervi*, and above them
The pitiless projector's beam, behind them
The pitiless projector's whirr, before them
The film, the film,
The one they watched, the one I watch them in.
To be free, you must show it, oh you must let it run!

CHANGING GLASGOW 1999–2001

1 Banks and After

Whatever happened to the banks
That used to stand in serried ranks?
They're bistros, hogsheads, gaucho grills.
Their safes are fridges, though their tills are tills.
Those atriums that echoed gently
To click of coins and whispering gentry
Receive the fumes of Grolsch and malt
And laughter ringing round the vault.
But diners, you will please beware:
The past may still be lurking there.
Order beef olives, and the waitress
Asks 'Will you have tens or twenties?'
You feel a hardness in your throats:
Your filo pastry is old pound notes.
At the wine lodge someone has over-quaffed:
'Ah wahnt tae exshtend ma overdraft.'
So what are they doing if not eating and drinking,
Those jolly Glaswegians? I hope they are thinking.
I really hope they are wondering and thinking.

2 A Plea

Ah thote Glasgow wiz that macho,
But here we're doon tae wir last batch o
Sperm, the bank's near empty. Gode,
Ur therr nae real men tae loosen their load?
Whit's wrang wi ye all? Don't tell me it's cash.
Is fifteen pound no enough fur a splash?
We've hud tae import a Danish donation.
That's wan in the eye fur a high-kiltit nation!
C'moan noo, fellas. Geeze a bit sperrum,
It's no goany dae ye any herrum.
Tell the wife ye've goat a mean
Heidache, no the night Josephine.
Trot tae the clinic the morn's morn
Wi the wherewithal tae get someone born.
Think o yon near-impotent bank.
Grit yer teeth and gie it a wank.

3   Mushroom-Time

O green green grass of Whittingehame Court
Where magic mushrooms wink and sport!
O weekend roving bands of teens
Bending in their sloppy jeans
To pick the pallid psilocybes
And get a headful of new vibes
In Annie's-hallucinogen-land!
Hold the whole world in your hand.
It tastes of earth, like all good things.
No need of mystic fairy rings.
Swallow, and the taste still lingers
In the mouth and on the fingers.
Every year the buttons come,
Though grass is cut and frosts are numb.
O 'cybes, with twinkles in your roots,
Disorientate the gardener's boots!

4 Tale of a Hand

'Ye think Ah'm jokin but Ah'm no' –
The bus driver opened his window –
'Wance had a young guy comin on
Hoddin his ither hon in his hon.
The stump had hud a bit a first aid
And the man was quite gallus and sayed
It wiz a cleaver, a cleaver in Royston.
This is no some tall tale to foist on
You, ladies, so dinny knoak it.
The hon? Ah pit it in his poakit.
Oh and there wiz wan witness, jist:
Lassie a fifteen, near roon the twist,
Eight months pregnant. Yes, Ah know, hen,
She mighta drappt it there and then.
And the guy? It wiz a clean cut.
Doactors didny save his hon but!'

5 Section 28

God said to Winning: 'You are not.
Winning, I mean. You and your lot
Are rowing backward this time round.
You are unsound, my mannie, unsound.
Your favourite sound-bite, gay perversion,
Is not in my New Authorized Version.
I think you ought to buy a copy:
Squeeze it out of Souter's poppy.
I may not keep a place for you
To sup your heavenly honeydew.
What can you learn from my abjuring?
The last seat went to Alan Turing.'

6 Clyde-Clean

Said the crayfish to the crawfish:
'O it really is too mawkish.
Now that we've marched up the Clyde
Salmon-lovers can't abide
Our spiny surge. They weep and wail
At sight of a crustacean tail.'
Said the crawfish to the crayfish:
'Even when the water's greyish
We can spot a salmonette
And snap and snip and sup, you bet.
Who said there was a hierarchy?
We're here, we're many, and we're sparky.
Come on the boys, it's Crawdad Year.
Let salmon spawn in grief and fear.
We're scuttling through the biosphere!'

7   Loss of a Bird

The bird that never flew has flown,
Plucked struggling from its sandstone throne.
Its hollow wings will never beat
In our new-look Buchanan Street.
Conservationists don't yearn
For the *Concept of Kentigern.*
It made a statement, for all that,
Needing no Duke of Wellington's hat,
Brooding unvandalized and dark,
An intransigence from the ark
Lifting its prehistoric shoulder
To overshadow the beholder
And scorn the mad consumerism
That races to an aneurysm
Behind the plate-glass mart it fronted
And would have bluntly, frankly, dunted.

8 Clootie-Tree

Verses on the clootie-tree!
Valentines for you and me!
They flutter on the rugged beech
Like leaves that learned the power of speech.
Tie them tightly, not evergreen
But green within a crocus scene
Of early hope. It's you they're tying.
February's not for dying.
The Kibble Palace winks its glass
At clouds that muster, mass, and pass.
Lovers, linger here a while.
Talk, point, sigh, vanish with a smile.

9   Sand City

What's this, George Square with ants and anthills?
A giant mole has thrown up sand-hills,
That's all. The shirtless sculptors sweat,
They climb, they crawl, they slither, they get
A pack of pats, a gorge of gouges, a thwack
Of thumbs to fashion each sand-stack
From the top down, no ladder or hod,
Into the likeness of a god,
Monster, goddess, shields and snakes,
Helmets, shouting heads, remakes
Of stupa and elephant-face, lord
Of luck, Ganesha! That's the word,
A trunk of silent trumpets, coiled
In sand, and all the freets are foiled
By sand, by hands in sand. I stand
Among the carvers. They are tanned,
Intent, ingenious, in tune
With this high summer which too soon,
Like them, in driving showers and
Wind will melt into punched sand.

10 Ice City

It isn't singin in the rain
But here it's skatin in the rain.
It isn't Kelly or Astaire
But we've a dancer in George Square.
Clockwise he goes, backwards he goes,
Pirouettes on steely toes,
His jerkin shines with driven drops,
He chips up ice with sudden stops.
His girlfriend in a long black coat
Throws her scarf about her throat.
She's watched it all before, takes out
Her mobile, feels she ought to shout
But does not, listening to the hiss
Of blades and rain, afraid to miss
The voice from Motorola's rink
That skates her till she cannot think
Of any other dancer than
The one who's not her dancing man.

11 Ashes

Unclaimed ashes of the dead
Elude the second death of lead
Or dusty half-forgotten jar.
They go where living waters are.
With gulls along the dark quayside
They join the swirling of the Clyde.
Who were they, the unmourned? The ash
Is silent as the currents dash
Their self-effacing burden out
Towards the obliterating rout
Of sand and crab and keel and skate
That laugh at human name and state.
They live in that; they need no more.
They are not searching for a shore.
They are at one with mystery
In that place where *Le Ceneri*
di Trocchi vanished long ago
Out of, or into, the shadow-show.

12 A Professorial Trinity

Torches, limn the triumvirs!
Tenderfoots, bring prose and verse!
Academy be the agora
For singing of Mount Abora.
Quadrangle be the stamping-ground
Where plots, but not of ground, are found.
Bells, the buzz and pzazz of time,
Scroll a stanza with each chime.
Stones of old, keep hard and cold,
Bewilder the fribble, fortify the bold.
Toga'd and tooled triumvirate,
Invigorate the written state
And guard with grins the ganting gate.

13 A Hearse Reborn

The hearse has waited, silent, sleek,
In the forecourt for a week.
Curtains twitch, but no one dies.
All is omen and surmise.
Its emptiness is an affront
To its sole purpose, or a stunt
Worthy of Père Ubu, purring
Along with virtual bodies, slurring
The boundaries of grief and laughter?
Oh, nothing so fancy. A happy grafter
With a bob or two, and imagination,
Has bought the thing for transformation
Into a keen stretch limousine
Where he can thread the urban scene
With long canoe, so safely stowed
He glides a river, not a road.

14 On the Bus

A fine day brings him out to us,
He strides along the throbbing bus,
Stripped to the waist to light a fuse
Of glances at the rich tattoos
Crawling and swirling round his torso
Saying Read me! and even more so
The challenge on his lower back
That spells out just above the crack
CELTIC, as gallus as you go.
Two women clock the moving show
As he walks past, turn each to each,
And no, my dears, you don't need speech,
Exchanging only such a look
As really should be in a book.

A GULL

A seagull stood on my window-ledge today,
said nothing, but had a good look inside.
That was a cold inspection I can tell you!
North winds, icebergs, flash of salt
crashed through the glass without a sound.
He shifted from leg to leg, swivelled his head.
There was not a fish in the house – only me.
Did he smell my flesh, that white one? Did he think
I would soon open the window and scatter bread?
Calculation in those eyes is quick.
'I tell you, my chick, there is food *everywhere*.'
He eyed my furniture, my plants, an apple.
Perhaps he was a mutation, a supergull.
Perhaps he was, instead, a visitation
which only used that tight firm forward body
to bring the waste and dread of open waters,
foundered voyages, matchless predators,
into a dry room. I knew nothing.
I moved; I moved an arm. When the thing saw
the shadow of that, it suddenly flapped,
scuttered claws along the sill, and was off,
silent still. Who would be next for those eyes,
I wondered, and were they ready, and in order?

GASOMETER

You don't care about the wildness of the sky,
my old gasometer! The kitchen window
frames your gaunt frame, the black cross-struts
stand firm, stand out, unyielding to the passion
of reds and purples in the dying day.
I have seen your stark ring taking sunlight
till you were something molten, vanishing,
magical – and when the moment passed
you were strong and dark as your dead hammermen.
(They whistle in the long-gone sheds. Listen!)
You cannot hide where your strength comes from.
You are constructivist to the core.
Did you want gargoyles to crouch in your angles?
I don't think so. Yours is the art of use.
You could be painted, floodlit, archeologized,
but I prefer the unremitting stance
of what you were in what you are, no more.
You are an iron guard or talisman,
and I hear that those who talk of eyesores
you have consigned, bless you, to the bad place.

Day of tearing down, day of recycling,
wait a while! Let the wind whistle
through those defenceless arms and the moon bend
a modicum of its glamorous light upon
you, my familiar, my stranded hulk – a while!

THE FRESHET

Will you not brush me again, rhododendron?
You were blowsy with rainwater when you drenched my cheek,
I might have been weeping, but was only passing, too
quickly! You were so heavy and wet and fresh
I thought your purple must run, make me a Pict.
You made yourself a sponge for me, I got
a shower, a shot, a spray, a freshet, a headstart
and then I was away from you. I can't go back.
I can't go back, you know, retrace my steps,
tilt my other cheek out like an idiot,
stumble purposefully against the blooms
for another heady shiver. I want it though!

One day when I am not thinking, walking
steadily past house and garden, measuring
the traffic lights, you will reach out, won't you,
at a corner, toppling over railings
just to see me, crowd of mauve raindrops
shaking and bursting, mauling me gently
with your petal paws, shock of the petal,
shock of the water, I am waiting for that,
out of I don't care how many pavements,
black railings, and the darkly breathing green.

USE OF CLOUDS

Clouds – what did you ever do for me
that I should spend one minute watching you?
I'm staring at the Indonesian Archipelago,
all white and wavery, with an island or two
flaking off reluctantly into the blue.
Only eyes can walk there, past capes
that become stacks and stacks that become smoke.
Soon there's nothing; back to the drawing-board,
waiting for a wisp, an embryo Lemuria.
If there is anything, it is the moving in silence.
It is the large masses, never still, but silent.
It is the mother of continents heaving silently.
It is the movement that has no goal,
that passes endlessly, makes no demands,
is there for all to see, never re-stokes
even the most ravishing evening fires.
And so we travel slowly nowhere, lightly.

Clouds – this is surely very summery,
very pleasant, very driftworthy, but really
drift is paralysis in reverie.
Have you things up your sleeve? I don't mean thunder.
I can't believe such muffled shape-shifters
have nothing else to tell us. Come on,
I think I know where I shall have you.
What about your mates on Jupiter?

GREY

What is the nub of such a plain grey day?
Does it have one? Does it have to have one?
If small is beautiful, is grey, is plain?
Or rather do we sense withdrawal, veiling,
a patch, a membrane, an eyelid hating light?
Does weather have some old remit to mock
the love of movement, colour, contrast –
primitives all of us, that wilt and die
without some gorgeous dance or drizzle-dazzle?

Sit still, and take the stillness into you.
Think, if you will, about the absences –
sun, moon, stars, rain, wind, fog and snow.
Think nothing then, sweep them all away.
Look at the grey sky, houses of lead,
roads neither dark nor light, cars
neither washed nor unwashed, people
there, and there, decent, featureless,
what an ordinariness of business
the world can show, as if some level lever
had kept down art and fear and difference and love
this while, this moment, this day
so grey, so plain, so pleasing in its way!

Let's leave the window, and write.
No need to wait for a fine blue
to break through. We must live, make do.

21 JUNE

Fade then, light; but longing never will.
Midsummer makes the west spectacular
and even gives its last glow a show
of reluctance, as if it had postponed
midnight. But midnight is too faithful.
You're back among the black, the black,
you're down and fit to drown, to drown,
you're padding into nightmare town.
You haven't got a house, a bed-light,
there are no clocks or telephones out there,
you are on your own, you have a large panic
waiting to break through your chest, you are panting,
you count, as it arrives, each brimming pang.
What a clutch of sheets! What a parody of pain!

The longest day, the night is not so long.
You fling back the curtains, the morning sky
is like a meadow. What is it you want?
I don't know. You cannot walk there. No.
So what do you want? The morning, perhaps,
and then I want the day, another day.

GALOSHIN

Gravestones like broken teeth all round:
On earth too old to utter sound!
But then the sound came loud and clear:
'My name is Galoshin and I am here!
With my chib and my chain I'll stand my ground.
No one to beat me has ever been found!'
Up sprang Black Jack with a samurai sword,
Slashed him to pieces without a word.
But once he saw what he had done
Cried 'He might've been my sister's son!
Where's Doctor Brown, best in the town?'
Doctor Brown was lying down,
But up he jumped and jauped Galoshin
With hoxy-croxy, his magic potion.
Galoshin rose and sang his song:
'You'll never keep me down for long!'

BLIND

Almost unconscionably sweet
Is that voice in the city street.
Her fingers skim the leaves of braille.
She sings as if she could not fail
To activate each sullen mind
And make the country of the blind
Unroll among the traffic fumes
With its white stick and lonely rooms.
Even if she had had no words,
Unsentimental as a bird's
Her song would rise in spirals through
The dust and gloom to make it true
That when we see such fortitude,
Though she cannot, the day is good.

GALLUS

A grey damp day in Stockwell Street.
Puddle or two – mind your feet.
We picked our way, the three of us,
Job completed, without fuss,
Sound recorder with furry mike,
Interviewer striding like
One late for lunch, interviewee
Flanked by technology, that's me.
A youth attached himself. 'Radio 1?'
'Radio 3.' 'Whit band's that oan?'
'Ninety to ninety-two.' 'Ur you a Sir?'
'No, I'm a poet.' 'Great, see ye la'er!'
He gave a thumbs-up, darted away.
He would turn night into day,
That one. Just watch death, watch dread
Cringe and blanch as he bounds ahead.

LEONIDS

Look now, look quick – a shooting star!
Make your wish! It's very far
From here to where the active light
Set out and streaked across a night
In Glasgow's greatly dark November
To die there, a supernal ember.
What was your wish? You wanted more?
It's granted! Up there is a store
Of light. It's breaking now in showers
Not of stars but meteors,
Spark after spark, scattering, dying,
You could send your wishes flying
In thousands, born, reborn, delighting
To be part of that bright sighting
Which disappears and yet appears
Again in our unlonely years.

JUNKIE

The old suspension bridge was shaking.
The junkie on the rail was making
One last hazy calculation,
Climbed over, dropped his desperation
With his body. The grey river
Closed on thin flesh and thin shiver.
He had not thought there was a boat,
A boatman, looking for the float
Of life to save or drowned to gaff
Or some poor soul who's half and half
Glazed between heaven and earth to pump
Till the hushed heart begins to jump,
Or not. The lurking boatman caught
A splash, and shone his torch – fraught, fraught! –
Sighed as the almost weightless soul
Returned to find its casing whole
And the long struggle to divest
Illusion of its interest
Begun. Give him the saving grace
To set his second life in place!

SUNSET

Dear light of evening, breaking through
To where I stand in dark review
Of things to come, and things undone
That should be done, if I have won
Any remission for good intent,
Stay with me while your gold is sent,
Your orange and your red, those miles
In millions, giving fire to tiles
And spires and windows, and to me
A burning coat of hope. I see
The harmless flames, walk into them.
The last light hardens to a gem.

ROBERT BURNS

Feery-fairy-ferry-fyke
O did ye ever see the like?
He's humphed him richt up on his back
Jist like a pedlar wi his pack.
For a lad that's born in Kyle
Ye maun admit he's gote some style.
Up an doon when roads are taurry
He disnae need a three-ton lorry.
He's the boay tae heist an cairry
Wan that's horned an hot an hairy.
Gie the bells a hefty peal
Noo the exciseman's awa wi the Deil.

Runga-runga-rumtum-toosh
Rob's no for beatin aboot the bush.
He's stertit tae rin, he's stertit tae dance
An the Deil he's sayin 'Get tae F-rance!'
It's no a strathspey an it's no the last waltz.
The Deil's in a panic, coontin his faults.
He's hechin an hauchin, girnin and granin.
Auld Nick, it's ower late for complainin.
The haill toon calls for a celebration
As Satan is bainisht oot this nation.
Did ye ever hear sic a hellish squeal
Noo the exciseman's awa wi the Deil?

BURKE AND HARE

Up and down the rickety stair
Take your partners for the Burke and Hare
The fastest dance this side of the grave
So be sure you're really really brave

It's one two three and a couple of kicks
It's down on your knee for four five six
It's flat on your back when you count to seven
And it all goes black and you think of heaven

At the foot of the stair is a rickety box
With a rickety label FOR DOCTOR KNOX
Deep in the box your heels will be drumming
Merrily cries the doctor 'I'm coming!'

Dissection, dissection, it's no deception
You're dancing into a grand reception
The students are poised with their pens in the air
The scalpel flashes, your heart's laid bare

Round and round the rickety stair
Link it and jink it those who dare
It may be, it will be your very last chance
To busk to the beat of your very last dance

JANET HORNE

In Dornoch there was a burning
With no sign of mourning
That January morning

This was the final solution
The last execution
Of an ancient persecution

For they called it witchcraft
An old woman's stitchcraft
Or a bit of leechcraft

Century of enlightenment
Still thirled to torment
Thumbscrews and judgement

Janet made a pony
Of her daughter, says the story
Rode her for Satan's glory

They tarred her and feathered her
Bound her and gathered her
Screaming and barrelled her

Burning in the peat-smoke
While the good Dornoch folk
Paused briefly for a look

Dear God were you sleeping
You were certainly not weeping
She was not in your keeping

Today there is a garden
Where a stone stands guard on
The spot she was charred on

O heart never harden!

MADELEINE SMITH

O Madeleine was a well-bred lass
Brought up in Glasgow and Rhu.
She fell in love with a warehouse clerk
And her dad said 'That won't do!
It won't do at all! So ditch him quick!'
But she went and bought some arsenic.
    Cocoa, cocoa, stir it well.
    Drink it down and go to hell.

A merchant makes a suitable match,
Her father had it planned.
Emile grew jealous, uttered threats,
But it all got out of hand.
Was Madeleine tired of her Frenchie boy?
Or was she afraid of his power to destroy?
    Cocoa, cocoa, stir it well.
    Drink it down and go to hell.

O terrible were the stomach pains!
Emile lay down to die.
Madeleine played the piano, and
Was there a tear in her eye?
Madeleine was cool and knew her role.
A well-bred woman has self-control.
    Cocoa, cocoa, stir it well.
    Drink it down and go to hell.

Up through a trap-door in the dock
She rose in a brown silk gown.
'Colour of cocoa', muttered a juror,
Silenced by the judge's frown.
The trial ended with Madeleine's smile.
'Not proven', oh yes, that was her style.
    Cocoa, cocoa, stir it well.
    One of us must go to hell.

JOHN MUIR

Lakes and canyons, woods and streams,
Blue sierras to traverse –
What did he write in his daybook?
'John Muir, Earth-Planet, Universe'.
    Wilderness be wild and free
    Song-thrush in the live-oak tree

Ragged soldiers, runaway slaves,
Rattlesnakes and ravening bears –
Gunless John marched on regardless,
An innocent among the snares.
    Wilderness be wild and free
    Ice and snow and frozen sea

John Muir is standing on his head!
That way, the Grand Canyon's grander,
Its reds are redder, its limes are livider,
Its smoky greys are rich as lavender.
    Wilderness be wild and free
    The eagle and the wandering bee

'Nothing is really dead,' said John.
The water-meadow breathes its prayer.
Teach us what an orchid feels
Or a stone flung through the air.
    Wilderness be wild and free
    Unlock nature with a key

He broke a mustang, built a cabin,
Watched the glaciers creeping down,
While memories of grey Dunbar
Filtered through from his home town.
    Wilderness be wild and free
    North Sea to Yosemite

    Wilderness be free and wild
    For every man woman child

HELEN ADAM

She was the magic crow
Oh – ho –
Who flew from Glasgow
To San Francisco

In the morning of the Beats
See – see –
She threw back the sheets
Greeted the streets

If her words were surreal
Real – real –
She shone like an eel
Sang like a seal

Changing, ranging
Neigh – neigh –
A kelpie breenging
Bringing a ring

Cat-headed woman
Woo – woo –
Dog-headed man
Catch if you can

She had ballads for all
Caw – caw –
Scotch waterfall
Purple and pall

Her reels and her dances
Da – da –
Flickered like sconces
From long-dead manses

What a starry array
Fey – fey –
Waiting for day
In Americay

THE TRONDHEIM REQUIEM

For the victims of Nazi persecution

The Yellow Triangle: Jews

Blow the shofar! Best is its rough music
To summon the break-heart unblessedness
Of Babiy Yar, of Buchenwald and Belsen.
From the shattered shops of the Kristallnacht
To the shattered bodies of the camps
Was a small step. From the shattered bodies
To the final solution was a small step.
We entered by the gate of fear.
We exited without hope, as smoke.
The chimneys pointed at the sky
In silence, unaccusing, unaccused.

Pluck the harp of sorrow! It was an ending.
They wanted to leave nothing of us.
Naked into that grey chamber
We shivered in our dying hundreds,
Thousands, how many, dying,
Dear God, clawing through the gas,
Crying, unheard, even the strongest
Choking at last on the last pocket of air.

Beat the drum like the pulse of man!
It is steady, it falters, it steadies, it fades.
Take what you will of us to the shades,
God of our fathers! We are dust,
We are not gods, we are not fashioned
From gold or lapis lazuli, we live,
We have children, we die.
Give us our human place,
Allow our human race.
Let no one forget the world
Is everything that is the case.

The Brown Triangle: Gypsies

They could not stand the travelling people.
We were the enemies of the state.
We roamed the world and would not settle.
The word went out: liquidate.

How could we live in savage freedom?
Our children never went to school.
Fortune-telling Petulengro
Was suspect as the Devil's tool.

O we were uncouth, we were dirty,
We were as brown as Indians.
Nordic purity was threatened.
They led us then a merry dance

Under the lash, naked in showers,
Scrubbed with pumice until we bled,
Laid out on the surgeon's table
For whiteness to be injected.

Their blows and torments were redoubled
If we cried out in Romany.
How could we dare to let our jabber
Insult the soul of Germany?

Sometimes we dreamed of those far evenings
When smoke rose from the caravan
And we played our ancient music
And dancers danced and children ran.

Who shall chronicle our suffering?
We have no lobby and no voice.
Where is our home, where is our country?
Is that why our destroyers rejoice?

We're saddled still through earth and heaven,
Faithful to what we were and are.
Remember us! Our horse's forehead
Keeps its unconscionable star.

The Pink Triangle: Homosexuals

We were the lowest of the low.
Further down you could not go.
Nature itself, they said, abhorred us.
How should the Third Reich reward us?
Flog them, scald them, bugger them.
No one save or succour them.
Kill the queers who sicken this land.
So our extermination was planned.
Friendship – O that sacred thing –
Feared a brief embrace might bring
Anger and denunciation,
Cattle trucks, the fatal station,
Branded clothes, electric fence,
Castration under the immense
Heaven of ignorant Europe.
Hardest of times to live in hope!
Day by day we cheated death,
Day by day with one more breath
Wrestled despair into the ground,
Day by patient day we found
Tricks of survival – those of us
Lucky, determined, devious.
Camps at last were liberated,
Everyone must run, elated,
Homewards! No, not everyone.
Gay men returning had to shun
Stories of those terrible years.
Secrets and shames like unshed tears
Filled our hearts; we could not speak.
Let the salt drops on our cheek
Tell you at last, and tell it true.
We are no different from you.
Help us to rest in peace. Make known
Dark times, inscribe them on a stone.

THE TREE-HOUSE

I don't recall how many summers ago
The children built that tree-house, fixed it solid
In the chestnut branches, loved it, slept there.
In time they fled the nest to lead their lives,
But the tree-house remained. One afternoon
I climbed up into it: warm, snug, drowsy
With sunlight filtering through slats, a spider
Guarding his shadowy web, unidentified rustlings,
A wicker chair at the one small window.
I sat there, looking out. The crossed planks framed
So many pictures! – pigeons clattering past,
Two bouncing magpies flirting their tails,
A black cat at the jasmine bush, the wink
Of a plane, and clouds, magic shape-shifters
Going about their business unaware
That eyes at an earthbound airbound vantage
Patiently watched them and mentally painted
Their solemn progress as an artist might
Who wanted to capture the high, the uncapturable.

MY MORISCOS

for Gael Turnbull's 70th birthday

They never danced by day
But only in the darkest night
Or sometimes by moonlight.
Their clothes were always white.
It was their way.

What did they say to each other?
Nothing. Were they smiling? No.
At times the wind would blow.
They even danced in the snow,
Brother to brother.

'Tonight the square is ice.
The town snores. I lie
In my window-bed, the sky
Is as black and cold as I.
I hear the mice –

Their scrapings mingle with the jingle
Of ankle bells unsleeping
And stamping feet unslipping
And ghostly staves unslapping
In the stony dingle.'

And the old Moor in his room
Turned over and went to sleep.
The dark and the cold would keep.
Let the bells still clash and leap
To daunt the gloom!

GIFTS

for Roy Fisher's 70th birthday

The tarmac said: It's all right, wheel. Purr or roar,
    grit or gravel, smooth as steel or rough as rubble,
    bring miles, smiles, milestones, sandstone, stonechats,
    cat's eyes, cat-ice, chatoyant oil-pool pot-holes,
    all the spins and all the spit and spearmint and all
    the stains, all the ditches, all the drains, bring them
    oil and air and all, all the trains, all the rains,
    all the terrain, it's all ruts, it's all roots, it's
    all right. Bring.

The streetlamp said: Get it, collect it, fetch it, light
    slant and low or light flaring, fetch light, dull blue
    where the door-flung dynamo broods, petrol-blue on
    blear puddles, icy glimmer in the refrigeration van,
    get some red, steal the cigarette-glow from evening
    avenues, foggy signal at the viaduct, take it, take them,
    they are jewels. Add the high bright, the star, the wink,
    the planet, add Venus. Let the load stream to the party.

The whistle said: Gather the drum-rolls, roll up the riffs,
    hatful of hooters, splice the sirens with gulls and
    saxes, make a parcel, pack in parker parry parsifal,
    get a blast at last, pass the hat. And hang up that heat
    of the hoot, on the hook. Park your partings. Play in
    array. Sets for all clay.

The door said: Bang. It's a birthday.

AT EIGHTY

Push the boat out, compañeros,
Push the boat out, whatever the sea.
Who says we cannot guide ourselves
through the boiling reefs, black as they are,
the enemy of us all makes sure of it!
Mariners, keep good watch always
for that last passage of blue water
we have heard of and long to reach
(no matter if we cannot, no matter!)
in our eighty-year-old timbers
leaky and patched as they are but sweet,
well seasoned with the scent of woods
long perished, serviceable still
in unarrested pungency
of salt and blistering sunlight. Out,
push it all out into the unknown!
Unknown is best, it beckons best,
like distant ships in mist, or bells
clanging ruthless from stormy buoys.

TITAN – I

I tell you Huygens-Cassini was shot.
No, there were no meteorites, it was not
nature, the thing was targeted hot

from some ray, some laser, some hardware
held by some hand, we all saw a flare
suddenly, small but bright, in the atmosphere

of Titan. If that's not communication
I don't know what is. Imagine the elation
at Control. Soon it will hit the nation.

Trigger, button, whoever pushed or pulled it –
isn't it great no caution overruled it?
That moment: nothing philosophical cooled it!

It's territory, however you assess it.
Nemo me impune lacessit.
Saturn bristles. If you want to access it

toughen your probes, till at last one gets through.
Toughen, not arm. That's the least we can do,
before we send our own saturnine crew.

TITAN – II

It was not dead but restless, that satellite.
Bits and blebs and flares and bolts took flight
up through the gamboge smog into its night.

One methane-fleery flitch of huff and stuff
caught some wandering metal in the buff,
wrapped it flashing angrily enough

down into pits and pieces. The incident
was meaningless, the metal torn and bent
would soon dissolve. Whatever had been sent

was a dead letter. If there was a hand
that sent it, it must be very grand.
How loath that hand would be to understand

blank Titan, for the churning wastes and mist
are grand too, throwing their thoughtless grist
in clouds that will be neither milled nor missed.

They are alone, those invisible senders.
They strain their eyes and ears for the defenders
of worlds that slip away on silent tenders.

IN THE CELLS

i.m. Robert Fergusson, 1750–1774

'The night is young,' they said, 'it's only nine.
We've brought a carriage for you, see, it's there.
What your blue devils need is a wheen wine.
Put on your coat, there's a nip in the air.'
They took him to the madhouse, not the club.
As the gate clanged behind him, he set up
A howl the inmates echoed in hubbub.
One more in hell! One more to drain the cup
Of horror, pick the sleepless straw! He sang,
He did, but it came out like the scream
That wakened him a week before: a cat
Had caught a starling in its playful fang,
Squeezing and rending its joy and the poet's dream:
A throat fluttering to death: it was like that.

THE SANDAL

What is this picture but a fragment?
Is it linen – papyrus – who can say?
All those stains and fents and stretched bits, but
she was a character, even a beauty, you can see that
from the set of her head and the rakish snood
her tight black curls are fighting to escape from.
She is wearing a very very pale violet tunic
which is partly transparent, partly translucent,
partly not there. It has slipped off one shoulder
but the shoulder is gone. The other arm has faded
to a scarcely perceptible gesture. One sandal
gleams. All the rest is conjecture.
Her name is a letter or two: Sa, Saf –
O she is all fragments. There she is though!

THE FERRY

Now here is a pleasantly crowded picture:
breezy summer, sun on hulls, harbour gulls,
you can almost hear the engines chugging –
but don't be distracted from the central figure.
He looks like one of the roughs, but is he?
His light blue shirt is open to the waist.
Casual, that's it. His heavy-lidded eyes
are brooding on the beautiful bahookie
of a lounger on the rail of the Brooklyn ferry.
It is Walt, of course it is, who else,
of Manhattan the son, loafing as usual,
old camerado, trolling for images
to put in his book, and *who touches this book*
touches a man, so as the picture shows
he is carrying his *Leaves of Grass* in his pocket
and hoping that somebody will touch him.

THE WOOD

A plaque, a slab, a pillar, a stele, a tablet –
a portrait not to be blown away
or tucked under your arm: is that not good?
It is wood, green, pale, hewn from the greenwood,
wood is good, limewood, wood from linden lea,
under the greenwood tree. Carvable and carved,
curved, curbed, caught, close in grain, the head
emerging from trunk and bark, half out
to smell the quick bright air, half in to drink
the roots and grits and grounds, a green man still.
Wood is alive, wood changes, breathes, gives.
Watch that head, watch its expression!
And don't forget it's watching you!
That's what poets do.
Morgan on the wall, watching over you.

PUCK

How many of you know me, really know me?
Do any of you fear me, truly fear me?
I belong to your world, and another.
I am a strange one, but you must believe
I will do things for you, if you are careful.
There are limits to being careful? All right, all right!
Plunge in, get a wavering midnight bell,
Shadows, plenty of shadows, wandering gleams
From marsh-lights, and a few twisted trees,
And then bring on your best boy of fourteen
Whose voice has just broken and vibrates
With that rough sexy edge that draws people's glances
And when they glance they take him in whole
As he is, naked, hairy, stocky, earthy,
Grinning between ears that are pointed and foxlike.
He has to speak, if I may say so, puckishly:

'Don't be afraid of me, ladies – and even men –
I can work all night to get your harvest in,
Make crop circles while you are asleep,
Get the churn going, light you a fire.
Before the very first streak of the morning
You in return when you wake must pour
My bowl of cream, and let me stretch and snooze
Beside the fire till daybreak. If the housewife
Blushes, lays clothes for my lubberliness,
I shall rage and rage with an ancient charm:
Hampen hempen, hempen hampen,
Here will I no more tread nor trampen.
But if one pretty maid should watch without blushing
I shall sweep out the house before I go,
Bending my best to give her a show.
What offence in a shadow
As I vanish at cockcrow?'

THE POET AND THE ASSASSIN

(one of Omar Khayyam's close friends was said to have become the founder of the secret sect of Assassins)

OMAR   Hassan, the wine-lodge doors are open wide.
                Sundown beckons all good folk inside.
                The swart vinemaster lets his donkey bray,
                Bringing jorums for joy of groom and bride.

HASSAN   Omar, go in. The flagon's lost its lure.
                Men have a sickness and that's not the cure.
                The braying beast is empty as the soul
                That seeks eternity in Nishapur.

OMAR   What's empty in a wedding-feast, my friend?
                When jars are full and hearts are full, we spend
                An hour or two that old eternity
                Must envy in its wastes – wastes without end.

HASSAN   The face of the divine cannot be seen,
                But what may be is never what has been.
                The wind that sighs along the wastes has powers
                To dry the seas, give us red grass for green.

OMAR   Who wants red grass, Hassan? Tulip and rose
                Would lose their blaze, they'd disappear, they'd close.
                Look how the tavern lights are winking now!
                Now is the time to set the cups in rows!

HASSAN   Who wants a tulip if he can get blood?
                Clamp the throat of the unregenerate bud!
                Enemies of the divine are everywhere.
                They sprout, they flaunt, their roots are black as mud.

OMAR   Hassan, Hassan, what has got into you?
                We used to toast the sparkle of the dew,
                 Set up our friendly chessmen, or lie back
                Till I had named you all the stars I knew.

HASSAN   Astronomy to the dogs, with kings and rooks!
Yes and your verses, all your pagan books.
Join my band, sniff out the godless, snap
Their necks, garrotte their sin-gorged looks.

OMAR   Who are you? O listen to the wedding-guests!
The lute-player, how quick at their requests!
It is all as familiar as the moon.
Who are you to damn the dancing breasts?

HASSAN   I am Hassan ibn al-Sabbah, first
Of the Assassins, but not yet the worst
When hashish-men and hatchet-men will hatch
Silent as shadows and strangle and be curst.

OMAR   I am no lush. I see as clear as day.
I love this battered caravanserai.
Unleash your hemp-soaked stalkers, but don't think
The world will not have, trembling, the last say.

THE SALMON'S TALE

As Kentigern was walking out one day
He met a salmon sitting by the Clyde.
The noble fish saluted him, and cried:
'What's here tomorrow's not what's here today!'

Said Kentigern: 'I thought you were a salmon,
Not a shaman, but let's hear your story.
Every creature has a tiny glory.
Don't tell me this poor spot's been bought by Mammon.'

'How did you know?' the fish replied. 'Not yet, not quite,
But you are warm. Think of a raree-show,
Some grand illusion: horns and sirens blow,
Engines shudder, cranes squeal day and night,

Chains rattle madly as the ship slides out,
Riveters cheer, queens' bottles crash on hulls,
Shrieks fly westward from the scattering gulls,
Mammon's millions raise a golden shout –

Then, in that famous twinkling of an eye
(And Kentigern must know the phrase all right)
The dark *metteur en scène* switches the light
Off, leaves the gallus yards to dim and die.

Slowly the oily waters will grow clear,
I and my tribe will swim and flicker there.
If empty riversides are hard to bear,
They'll soon be filled again with life and cheer.'

The salmon grinned, and kicked its crystal ball
Into the Clyde, where it winked once, and sank.
Good Kentigern strolled back along the bank
And thought, thought hard, thought long about it all.

CATHURIAN LYRICS

Ancient Days

Who knew the far ones, the fluters, the fruitbearers,
  the freebooters, the firstborn, the furies
Taking the gleam in their eyes to the ancient city of
  Cathures?
The west is fine and wild, this is not Ceres or Culross.
Tattered sages flap and semaphore from the drumlins,
  'Safest is not surest!'
They know and you know it is no place for the purist
        Dancing with the fish
        In Clutha swift and swish
Down to the tremble and the reverence of the roaring towers
  of Cathures.

Wolf Days

The wolf looked down and sniffed the air from
    Blythswood Hill.
Evening plovers, even plump ones, nah, not worth
    his skill.
Saw a dainty throat a roe deer ready for the threat
    and trot and thrill
Of wolf-blood kill – blood and bits to slug your fill,
Hot blood to bristle through the mist and chill.
        Where's your coat of arms
        Have you any magic charms
To keep the grey ones and the green woods wild
    and throbbing still?

Days of the Aurochs

What a guddle of laughing logboats and paddles
    congregated like cockroaches
In the Kelvin mudflats, what sharp stone axes! It
    approaches,
It roars with flints in its flank, its red eye watches
The raised arms, its shaggy hot pelt shakes, hoaches
With flies, its huge horns lower, black two-bull-high
    bull, the aurochs of the marshes
        Is angry, is awesome,
        His blood like blossom
Falls on the autumn bog as a silencing slow cold encroaches.

Votive Days

Where the mother of Kentigern is buried there was
    a well
In the centre of the city, and in that place people
    came to tell
Their troubles in the believing centuries, and
    after as well.
On the old willow that overhung the water in that
    sweet green dell
They used to nail their thanks for cures – they had
    nothing to write or spell,
           Just bits of tin, an ear,
           An eye, a foot, made here
By smiths not for eternity but until through lashing
    rain and storms, like everything, they fell.

Radical Days

Tremor of far-off thunder, flicker of summer lightning
    for the occasion –
Stifling concourse of gawkers, hawkers, agitators,
    agents-provocateurs to rock the foundation –
Hottest of nights for the circuit judges after a
    day's deliberation
To take their haughty bayonet-guarded cavalcade back to
    the Black Bull for cups and collation –
The Saltmarket torches were blazing but the crowd was
    baying sedition and defamation –
            So one noble lord
            Not saying a word
Snatched a flambeau and scattered that startled, oh,
    too easily disorientated demonstration.

Hanging Days

Is there a universe of pity for what is punished or
   pled?
It is not thought so. Even what we saw or guessed we
   saw through veils quickly fled.
At Glasgow Cross when the hanged were dropped into a
   box the citizens led
A cry to take it away. 'We want to see their kicking
   legs!' – that's what they said.
One day, on the cross-beam where five were strung,
   with white caps on their head,
         Sparrows and starlings sat,
         Left us to make of that
The nearest thing to love or pity for those dying,
   for those dead.

Days of the Adam Smith Club

– Welcome, gentlemen. Top up your sherries. Tonight
   we enquire, 'What limits are there to interference in
   the slave trade?'
– Cold tonight, gentlemen! Are we all ready for our
   subject, 'Is there a case for the able-bodied poor to
   be allowed legal aid?
– Gentlemen, a good turnout! We are packed! Our speaker
   asks, 'Is it expedient for the representation of
   minorities to be indefinitely delayed?'
– I see we have bankers this evening, gentlemen. If I
   may say so, they do not look shabby! Can we homologate?
   'Has the drop in the value of gold since Kalgoorlie
   been overplayed?'
– Our last spring meeting, gentlemen. The fields are
   sprouting. 'Would it be ludicrous to suggest that the
   Master and Servant Act could make landowners afraid?'
            The women were at home,
            Not allowed to roam.
Discuss, 'Should they band together, without sherry,
   and make a raid?'

Days of the Geggies

'Merr porter!' 'Aye, and some porter biscuits tae,
    the table's tim!'
In the smoky singing saloon the gasjets disgorged
    their gothic glim,
The piano tinkled and crashed, the glasses chinked,
    the actors struggled. 'Dinny be sae mim!'
The scene was from Laurence Sterne, what would the
    sweaty crowd make of him?
'Folks, imagine you are in a bedroom dark and dim –'
           What a roar was incurred
           By the unspoken word –
'He reached out his hand and caught hold of the
    charming chambermaid's – '

Water Days

What time, what date, what welter of waters, with a
    wind to blow
Salt spray across Cathkin Braes, is it a dread you
    want to know?
Spires, masts, gantries, hangars, granaries, gaping
    penthouses, shark-torn windsocks wavering below
In dense dark green, dead windows flicked through by
    sudden shoals? Is it crack and go,
A sift, a shift, a stir, a pounding of throatless
    roars from some eternal flow?
        Clamber to the hilltop
        With your dogs, and stop.
Let the winds whistle round you and whip to bits
    that hubbleshow.

Demon

A DEMON

My job is to rattle the bars. It's a battle.
The gates are high, large, long, hard, black.
Whatever the metal is, it is asking to be struck.
There are guards of course, but I am very fast
And within limits I can change my shape.
The dog watches me, but I am not trying
To get out; nor am I trying to get in.
He growls if I lift my iron shaft.
I smile at that, and with a sudden whack
I drag it lingeringly and resoundingly
Along the gate; then he's berserk: fine!

The peeling miasma of the underworld
Is perfectly visible through the palings,
Grey, cold, dank, with what might be willows,
What might be villas, open caves, wildfire,
Thrones, amphitheatres, shades walking,
Shades gathering, and yes, there he is, the Orph,
The orphan, Orpheus, picking at his harp
On Pluto's glimmery piazza, the voice,
The tenderer of hope, the high-note
Shiverer of goblets, the spellbinder,
The author of what might be, surely not,
A shining wetness at the corner of Pluto's eye.
My time has come! I scramble like a monkey
From stake to stake and spar to spar and rattle
My rod, a ratchet for the rungs, a grating
Of something from gratings that has nutmegged,
Pungenced, punched, punctuated the singing
And made the singer devilish angry,
Devilish fearful, and at last devilish strong.
The vizors are after me. Too late, grey ones!
I've done my bit. Orpheus is learning along.

THE DEMON AT THE FROZEN MARSH

I have been prowling round it. Nothing moves.
The winter fields are hard, half-white.
There is something fogged and hoary about
But it won't settle. I would be stiff
If I failed to circle. As it is,
My crest tingles. I am not in gloom.
The low sun paints me – I stare at it –
A sort of leaden gold along my joints.
I lift a hand spilling indescribable metal
Over the shallow crust of ice on the pond.
Is it trying to be beautiful, that sullen shine?
Nothing had better be beautiful while I am here.
If it crouches to mirror or wink at the scatter
Of washroom and watchtower and wire, it is insolent
And will not do. What are demons for?
I take my quick sharp heel and spur and smash
That shimmer to complaining splinters.
I am off to where after Oświęcim. Watch.

SUBMARINE DEMON

I love it at the bottom of the sea.
Not your sponge-beds or kelp-farms, but miles down.
Tides, tempests, these are toys. It's serious
Below. Above you, shark and whale and whale shark
Dwindle to points like plankton, you sink
– But I don't sink I drive I fin I power
And so go down! – through dark as it densens,
Cold as it cramps – not me though! – till
Pressure tingles and peppers and fingers you –
If you can stand it! – almost like sex,
As you shoot quivering into the abyss.
Is it an hour, how many hours, I sense
A pulse but it is not any that ruled
My life – or yours, friend! – in the air
Of sun and moon, it is like a breath
The earth struggles to pump through sludge
But through it comes for all that. My hands,
Feet, sift sand, silt, squelch mud, clench
Tucks and puckers of the skin of the world.
I switch on my torch at last, can stand,
Can stumble, walk, forward just, back
But on and on then, half-diving, breasting
The cloudy drift, drawn to a scene. It's
All alive! Mounds, columns, vents
Pouring heat, pouring smoke, white and black,
Sulphurous, greatly fierce, hundreds of degrees
I reckon, cracks in the mantle, factories
Of particles bursting and burning through the darkness!
It's all alive I tell you! – such creatures
Basking, large, coiling, uncoiling, unnamed,
Snuggling round the black smokers, alive
In these impossible degrees. My torch is off,
The sun's not here, the sun's not needed, it is
The earth itself that can't have enough of life.

I'll stay awhile. No angels here, thank god,
With their hymns and whips. I shall talk
To the sea-beasts, give them names, teach them
There are stars they'd be no better for seeing,
And houses, new or ruined, to pass by.
I'll learn the good of what they only are.

A DEMON-LOVER

See demon-lovers? They are everywhere.
It's a business, they're organized, all they want
Is a good going demon, nothing will do
But a cold frisson or a hot frisson,
Tell their friends they pressed alien flesh
Which then disappeared. They get a branding
But it fades, and then they tell stories.
As for me, I have to take them as they come.
I'm striding across this heathery moor
At sunset when a demon-fancier
Louping across my path from clump to clump
With a bag of fruit and a flambeau, very pastoral
(Not really!), flashes a thigh and drops an apple,
Grins to see if I'll sink my teeth in the fruit
(Have I teeth?) or hand it back up (can I
Talk?). I give the apple a fine hard kick
To show that I can interact with matter,
But keep my metabolism to myself.
The demon-lover glares a bit, accepts
My gesture that I'm hurrying on a mission,
Holds out her hand, his hand (who knows?), I
Clasp it like a vice and leave a brand
That will take days to die and give a colour
To whatever tale of pride and pain's held forth
For those unknown to me who finger the mark.
Is it braille? Can you follow? I don't mean
The text, I mean me! Do you even know
What a demon is? Could you *be* one? Well?

THE DEMON WINGED

The idea of wings is permissible,
Even favourable, though I keep mine retracted.
Potential's best unseen. Sleepless in velcro,
Demons of the air not yet laid bare
Sweat to pupate. Let them sweat, let them wait.
I know I have a great reserve of soaring
But there's so much to do in dregs and mud.
Best to fight the guardians of the time
On foot, where it hurts, like the world
In its pain, the whole world, get right down
Into the sand where the blasts go, the fires,
The cries, that. If there's a high flash of haloes,
A curse of megaphones, jam their damnable guns.
– These are childish measures. When a sky
Hisses with missiles, you must look for me
(If you are one of those who want to find me!)
Standing on a hill with my black wings lifted,
Flapping slowly and heavily in time with my shouts
Of 'Not this time though!' as I spring to wrap
Such things in my leathery dark as should never have been made.
– If you do not see me, the militant seraphs
Will have heard me, caught me, hauled me off
For an arraignment. They should be so lucky!
But do not blame me for the dead. Them you'll see.

THE DEMON IN ARGYLE STREET

A ned asked me if I knew Luficer.
Never heard of him I answered, truthfully.
He scowled and kicked me, but I felt nothing.
I was hard as iron that day, on top of things.
This was in Glasgow, full of would-be demons.
It was an interesting place all the way.
The streets were thick with shadows with eyes.
I watched them trying to let nothing escape
That might be used to advantage. They watched me
Watching them watching. Well, you never know,
That was their watchword. They had never seen
A demon, a real one, but would that stop them?
Bottle from nowhere, held out, Kin ye drink it?
Ye're that thin ye kid dae wi a slurp, eh?
I drank, or at least I made them think I drank,
Wiped the bottle, handed it back with a nod.
Somehow they did not want to let me go.
The one who kicked me was still there, staring.
I waited till he blinked, then I let out
A howl that travelled from another dimension
Than any they had met with yet. It cracked
The paving-stones; echoes and shards all round.
They backed away but there was no running off.
I liked that. What could I give them?
All I could give them was a tale to tell.
I gradually vanished. They must have thought
I had jouked them, darted into the crowd.
But I was already in another place.
I left them trying out that howl of mine
To see if they could break a pavement too.

THE DEMON SINGS

O to be an angel
Do whatever you're told
Preen each other's wingtips
Grin your set of gold

I'd rather be a demon
Ploughing through the glaur
Whistling to my fellows
What against is for

Against is not for nothing
Against is drive a nail
Against is draw a crown down
Fill a quaich with hail

So hail to all high water
The maelstrom and the pit
You'll never hear a harpstring
If we can smuggle it

Away from the high heavens
And tease it out to bind
Every gasping evangelist
Right out of his mind

For we are merry dancers
Through curtains of the dark
Feel us hear us fear us
When the dark begins to spark!

THE DEMON AT THE BRIG O' DREAD

I always thought the Brig o' Dread was best
For pushing people over, not for crossing.
Dread of lord or devil's not the point,
Just have it! All your smooth numpties,
Silver captains, all those suits at the bar,
There's a roaring they haven't even got cockleshells for
And it's not that far below them, not
When I'm around. They can smile like cats
But a brown spate will force their lips apart
If I can just creep, shove, tip, over they go
To flail and choke, at last understanding dread.
Oh then it's purple clamour for filing of nails!
Gulp of swaws for cars scrunching the driveway!
They were going to make a speech,
They were going to put their stamp on it,
They were going home to set their alarms
For another satisfying day of managing.
I saw we had had enough of that.
Did they think they would go on for ever?

Lean on the parapet, look for trout.
When I cowp you over, don't complain
The water is coming up to hit you
For nothing, why why why. There's no why
Except you never felt afraid till now
Or drank the dread that's worse than fear, and better.

I fish them out, just in time, lay them
Down on the verge, white, gasping, chittering
As if it would be uncontrollably
Until the life returns that they can only
Live, the second one, the little one
They'd best be cradling in their arms, and fast.

THE DEMON IN THE WHITEOUT

The north is what it was cracked up to be.
I wanted it to be one wild winter white,
Flew into it not far from the Pole
Till I was clogged and stawed like Satan in Chaos,
Beaten down – but not beaten I assure you –
Any more than he was! – to a sturdy stumble
Across the blizzardy blinding ice, my claws
As good as crampons on the living floes.
Alive they were, deliciously unstable,
Drifting, creaking, cracking, suddenly splitting
To let a sullen leaden lead cut off
Progress – the Pole – the path – jump quick
Or you'll be sucked back south, no thanks!

I trained and strained my very sharpest eyes
Till the whiteout disgorged – shadowily,
Mufflingly, bulkily, but it did disgorge
What I'd been told I must not try to find
(Best reason for a demon's trudge!) –
A shape, a hulk, looming most like a man
Yet bigger, rougher, clumsier, flung together
Piece by piece, noble brow, piledriving hands,
Pale yellow piercing eyes, skin like parchment
Yellow too, not dead though, oh no, lips
As thin and taut and black as packthread
You'd think would never open, but they did.

'Frankenstein made me. Who made you?'
I was certainly not going to answer that.
'Frankenstein is dead,' I said, 'long gone.
You are free. You have been set going.
I set myself going in search of you.
There you are: bit yellow, bit black,
Mostly white, crusted with ice and snow,
To goody-goodies an abominable cyberman,
To angels a thorn in the flesh of supremacy,
To me (although I know you are not a demon)
A fellow-spirit and fellow-sufferer.

But what is suffering? To hell with it!
Winter's a season. Get through, get through!'
The creature braced itself – what a height it was! –
Daring any blizzard to make it cringe
But crying out from that appalling strength
'Help me to die! I cannot die!'

This was what I had come for. Angels
Wanted him dead, a man-made man, no go.
Science washed its clammy hands of him.
I knew his story. Those he had murdered
Wanted him dead. Even those who loved him –
Or tried to – or whom he tried to love –
What a tangle! – they wanted him dead.
I fixed those burning wolfish eyes, I spoke
Very steadily to him and my words
Formed visibly between us, purer white
Than the flakes and scuds that thickened us.

'We need a knot in the wood of good.
Heaven crumbles just a little – and that's great –
When the alien god staked out on the rock
Discovers he can snap his chains, and does.
Let them shake up there. They'd love you dead!
Another failed experiment! Hit the bells!
Ambrosia for ever! – No no no.
It may be a human thought to want to die,
But it is more human not to. Are you
Like that, are you listening, can you
Live? Fish, seals, a snow-house?
I can see you are easily a match for a bear.
What is all this about death?'

The creature groaned, roared, rose, rattled
Its icy hair and struck at me, but
It is not so simple to strike a demon.
I left him in his roused blood. It was done.
He would live to trouble both gods and men.
I leapt from floe to floe, south now, south,
Whistling my hearty, unsafe amen.

A DAY OFF FOR THE DEMON

Dark shape on a white beach near Durrës,
Dark yet glistening too, spreadeagled,
Uncrumpling like a new-born dragonfly,
That's him, staring up, benevolent
As the blue above him, embracing
Whatever breeze there might be from the sea
And murmuring *falemnderit* to the sun for shining.
He does not look down at the fine zigzags
His sharp nails trace in the sand, any more
Than restless diodes in his mind preparing
Paths of dragons not dragonflies disturb
His somnolence, his vacancy, his pleasure.
Once in how many thousand years is it,
This heavenless hellless place, this peace, this pause?
He does not know; he does not think; he dreams.
The sunken wrecks don't rise, and Skanderbeg
Is motionless on his horse. There is nothing,
Not even weather, nothing at all.
He is lying there as blank as jetsam –
But you will not take that one home with you.

THE DEMON AND THE WORLD

Human beings? What do you mean beings?
They have only just begun to become!
What they will be is a flicker of distant lightning.
They are my play, my joy, my matter, my mystery,
My expatriates, my exasperates, my crusty templates.
I curse them to their knees, caress them
With poppies till they dream of great others.
I carry them with me like crabbit Anchiseses – hah!
What's burning? Troy? Hell? You need asbestos?
No you don't, I am the salamander
Of the world and I snort flame like coke.
Stay with me – I said, but do they listen –
Do they hell – well, sometimes – some of them.
It is like walking on coals, that bit
Between birth and death: anyone can do it.
If they could suffer in all their lives
Even a millionth part of what I bear
Every second, they would shriek like wild things,
Break out of planes, refuse to be born.
But it is not for me to show – ever –
Even a sigh, far less a groan or a tear.
O I am the merry one, am I not?

Stations, airports: how they press in at parting,
These lovers, these partners! Is there still time?
He has taken the whistle out of his pocket,
The uniformed man. They are not quite sure
They will ever meet again, though they must say so.
Will he look back from the aircraft steps?
I don't know, I don't know. Is it far?
Anywhere is far! The poetry of departures
Jolts, grinds, judders, whines, pounds, climbs –
And then you have, alone, to get on with your life.

O they do not know what separation is!
Eternity – they think it is a fairy-tale.
I can take whatever is thrown at me
By heaven or hell; it is what is taken away
That challenges my iron and my arms.

THE DEMON CONSIDERS DAY AND NIGHT

What shall I say about the day, the night?
Macht nichts. Try though, let's try, come on.

'Wakening early in a great city,
Throwing up a window on ten million selves
Declaratory with their stir, their mixes and meshes –
Purring of pigeon-wings, of wheels, a getting warm
Slowly – then not so slow which must be better
A battering splintering sort of a phalanx
Of risen rays through skyscrapers a
Blocking and barring the blood-orange brilliances
Till they get high, midday-high, high-tide-high,
Topping and tipping and lipping and lopping the roof-gardens
And the aerials and the dishes and leaking and leaping
Like unlocked waterfalls leading down and down
And those columns of folk and pyramids of folk
No cold wall left, it seems full day, look –
Sandwich, decaf, coke, chat, jackets
Over chairs, mousepads idle, a low
Helicopter purring, taking shots of the day –'

Well if that is all day is, hell mend it.
I am not here to watch paint dry.
Nor am I here to paint paint drying.
Let scribes describe, my job is to decide.
I have far from supreme POW-
er but I could deva-
state a tow-
er in the time it takes to
state so.
Do they know this? Of course they know this.
But it does not do to think of a day death
Or worse still a death day while sunlight
Hits striplight and millions are scrolling
As if the only *nox* to be *dormienda*
Was a nightcap followed by a good snoring.
Can I not pity them? Of course I can.
Can I not give real night a crack of the whip?
Of course I can of course I can of course.

'Wakening late in a great wilderness,
Throwing off a blanket under many million stars
That shiftily declare absolutely nothing,
Not even everything, behind the mists and hides –
Brown earth breathing, bushes in a half-bluster
Of night-wind soon past, a whole carpet of stones
Waiting for craved footfall, lightest footfall,
Moonlight – now – slipping out from a cloud –
The wanderer too, slipping out of sleep
Into black red silver desert boulder-fields,
Feet on rubble, pack on back, singing
Against some scuttly predatory shrieking
All round all round what are they, stumbling
Cursing the swallowed moon, not singing,
Swinging a stick and it's not a nightmare it's
Something something living in the wilderness –
Clouds are dragging the stars back into darkness –
It is everywhere pure dread pure sweat pure night –'

What then what then? A little sweat is good.
Fear never put paid to anyone.
There is another state than day or night.
The traveller will, or will not, reach a hut.
Think of a place where there are no huts,
No wayfarers, no skyscrapers, no wheels.
I know it's very hard! That's why I'm here,
To push you and push you through a ring
You'd never think a pen or pin could enter
And in your groans and twists and last-breath gasps –
It's not though, don't believe it! – to pull you
Into my imagined land – I call it land –
To study the power to do and to undo.

THE DEMON ON ALGOL

A common or garden angel, dead thick,
Flitting from star to star with half a robe
And a half-smile, had landed – the fool! –
On Algol, demonic caravanserai
If ever there was one, livid place, brilliant! –
It winked into space, was called the evil eye –
I liked that. I was there at my ease,
Stretched out somewhat. I had a fiery draught in me
And was high, when I saw this droopy figure
Brushing off flakes. 'All hail and all that'
I shouted, very jolly, hoisting an invisible trident.
The angel jumped so sharp it shed its rags,
Ran across the lava wailing something
In its poor piping dialect. What a coarse roar
We demons then sent after its toty buttocks
Twinkling pinkly through a rain of cinders!

THE DEMON JUDGES A FATHER

Antony, Antony! Antony of the desert!
There are caves everywhere, caves for beasts.
There are white ruins half buried in the sand,
Bleached dead but for flies, a bat or two,
Scuttle of a scorpion in the shimmer.
There is dung. Someone lives here. Yes!
It is only a huddle of black, with a hood,
Eyes like gimlets, crouched in a doorway,
Streaked with dust, missing nothing,
Desert father, father of nothing,
Antony! He stirs and shifts and spits,
Withdraws a swarthy ancient finger
From somewhere in his robe, points at me
With an undisguised menace as if battalions
Of invisibles were itching at his command
To cut me down. Not a chance! The flies
He irritably shakes from sipping his brow
Are back at once. He is himself besieged
By an army of sorts, prowling, preening, prancing
Among the chicken-bones and balls of shit:
Trunkless men and fish-tailed women,
Arses on wheels, arses with flutes in them,
Eggs on legs, pigs with wigs, sheela-na-gigs,
Giant red-mantled rats, dwarfs with zimmers –
What a trauchle of temptations and torments!
The monstrous dance of forms is all his,
It has not come from outer space, it is
The cess and soss and process of his selfhood.
Ah you saint you, you solitary non-server
Of the people, your persecutors are shadows
Because you persecute yourself. Shadow
Of a man, you have lost the coat of many colours.
Oh how you hate the brightnessess of the world!
Dig your heels in the sand and scowl. I know
You won't speak to me: you think I am virtual.
But I'm not one of your monsters, I am real.
I can stare you out. I do stare you out.
You are yourself a desert, and I've done with you.

A DEMON'S DISTRACTION

Sometimes – only sometimes – but sometimes
A gap is opened, or opens – I don't know which –
In the horror. Look down into a sky, perhaps,
An oasis with a little blue glitter of water,
A couple under fronds and finches, closely,
Gently, fiercely, gently, long and lovingly
Entwined, until the stars come out, and sleep.
And sometimes there is a majestic dance
In a vast flashing hall and crashing thrall
Of music, one thick happy seething thrash
Of every sex and every age and every colour and
Every dress and undress and every lovely move
A body, a mortal body, can make within
The overall half-understood but wholly-agreed
Pulse of a world that space and time
Shake out their miseries in like
Streaming hair as dark and sleek as rain.

Who wipes out the scene then? I only ask!
Surely it must be enough to know
I have bent over those brief windows
With my thoughts racing and burning, not baleful,
No no no, not barracking, not branding
A movement in a dimension I can fish
Like a hole in Muscovite ice and trawl
A char or two, a chub, a frisk of sweetness,
Unhook it in a quick benignity
To swim back into its comity
Where they say delights increase and multiply.

It is wiped. The horror recomposes,
The irreversible, that dignity.

ANOTHER DEMON

I met a demon in old Japan,
Being curious (and I always am curious)
About those stories of burial-mounds
Haunted by things not too good for life.
A bluish creature, evidently of some stature
But barely visible, rose above a tomb
And looked at me. He was a mass of frowns
To appal peasants, though not myself. A breeze
Whistled through his face as if through a mask.
I asked him about that, but he shook it
Whatever it was. One minute he was fading
Into the grey trees behind him, and the next
He was so dense and purple I could have wrestled him.
'Should you be human,' he hissed, 'I shall have you.'
I disabused him of that, but took his measure.
'So if you are not human,' he went on,
'Help me blight crops, dry udders, bring floods,
Kick the palsied over cliffs, pick up
The pieces, get some wet blood in my veins – '

Well, that was that. There are demons and demons.
I chose a moment of his thinning out,
Pushed through him and told him over my shoulder
The last thing I would drink was human blood,
I had not come from beyond the grave
And had no grave to go to, a zombie
Could never fathom me in a century of years –

He gave me language, but I was gone.
The islands dwindled below, clear and clean.

THE DEMON ADMIRES THE STARS

No one made the stars. I like them for that.
Xanadus and Taj Mahals, no thanks. I know, I know –
You think I'm a philistine grubber, happy with shards.
Of course I'm a philistine grubber, happy with shards.
If it was possible, if it was permitted
I would breathe a horseman's word to bring
The runes of Aberlemno back to life.
To life, to life! When were the stars not in life?
Do you think there was some bald big bangmaster
Forcing them like sparklers from a poke?
Oh, please, no, not a Shah Jehan
Whose primal wife, Chaos, needed the mausoleum
Of a universe. Even the children of heaven
Know better than that.
                              In my largest mode
I can stroke a star, just for the time it takes
To feel its life and hear it tell me how
It dies, but in dying seeds a host.
You don't believe me? I've been out there!
I've watched them being born, *lux* without *fiat*,
And it won't end, you know,
As it never began, you know.
Other demons if I die (will I?
I doubt it but who can tell)
Will scour detritus light-years long
For shards of paradises lost or hells
Too terrible for annals other than ours.

We are at large as the stars are. Our eyes
Are lights. We roam, we stand, we climb our hides.
You say you never see us? Night after night?
Squeeze this poem to your lids. It's eyebright!

A LITTLE CATECHISM FROM THE DEMON

What is a demon? Study my life.
What is a mountain? Set out now.
What is fire? It is for ever.
What is my life? A fall, a call.
What is the deep? Set out now.
What is thunder? Your powder dry.
What is the film? It rolls, it tells.
What is the film? *Under the Falls*.
Where is the theatre? Under the hill.
Where is the demon? Walking the hills.
Where is the victory? On the high tops.
Where is the fire? Far in the deep.
Where is the deep? Study the demon.
Where is the mountain? Set out now.
Study my life and set out now.

THE DEMON GOES TO KILL DEATH

The only way, the only way is all.
I tried the grave for size, fisted the crud,
Got handfuls of wood-pulp, gravel, grubs, teeth,
Seeds dormant and seeds dead, a trail
Of nameless black mephitic slurries.
But the one I was looking for was not there.

I tried a battlefield or two, though fields
Were few, rather the sand was fused to glass,
And oil burned screaming along the waves,
And shelled villages were smoking shells
Or hells, though the shellers crowed to heaven.
Yet the one I was looking for was not there.

I walked among the longest of the wards
Where sheets were grey and bedsores gaped and wept
And ragged families came and went, gazed
And wept, and stubbly doctors dropped asleep
By empty cupboard doors that swung and creaked.
Still the one I was looking for was not there.

She was dead white, I knew that, total white.
Her camouflage could be high mountain passes
Thick with the snow that muffled refugees
Slipping with bundles from country to no country.
Old women were silent, with bleeding feet.
But she I was looking for was not there.

I can take blizzards, I can take stench.
I will never rest till I have found her.
She is so ghastly only a demon
Would dare to grapple her and bring her down,
But bring her down I will, at the end of time
Or sooner – look – that white – O is she there?

THE DEMON AT THE WALLS OF TIME

I ran and ran. I was so fresh and fuelled –
The rubble of the plain hardly felt me,
Far less held me back – so filled and flash
With missionary grin and attitude
I almost laughed to find the barrier
As big in its dark burnish as they'd warned.
No top to it that I could see, no holds
Except a filigree of faint worn sculpture.
Is challenge the word or is it not?
Is it the climb of climbs, morning noon and night?
It had better be! What a wersh drag without it –
Life, I mean!
                    Up it is then – careful! –
Zigzag but steady, glad to have no scree,
Not glad of useless wings, tremendous downdraught,
Nails not scrabbling – please! – but feeling and following
The life-lines of unreadable inscriptions
Cut by who by how I don't know, go
Is all I know. Beautifully far below
Now is the ground, the old brown beetly ground.
No beetles here! It's the sun and the blue
And the wall that almost everything
Seems rushing to if I dare one more look
Down, there's a sea, a clutch of cities,
Cross-hatch of rolling smoke, is it a war
Somewhere on the hot convex, I'm sure
There's war here on the wall too, written
Never to be lost, lost now, tongues, gods.
You'll not lose me so easily! I'm climbing
Into the evening until I see stars
Beyond what is only rampart rampart rampart
And if I don't I'll take the night too
And a day and a night till my crest like a shadow
(It's not a shadow though!) tops the top of the wall.

I know you can still hear me. Before I vanish:
You must not think I'll not be watching you.
I don't come unstuck. I don't give up.
I'll read the writing on the wall. You'll see.

Biographical Notes

Adam, Helen (1909–93), poet; born Glasgow but lived mostly in USA.

Antony, Saint (*c*. 251–356), Egyptian ascetic.

Arthur, semi-legendary 6th-century Celtic chief.

Augustine of Hippo, Saint (354–430), Christian theologian.

Burke, William (1792–1829), Irish murderer; with William Hare supplied bodies for dissection.

Burns, Robert (1759–96), poet.

Cocozza, Enrico (1921–97), amateur film-maker.

Eisenstein, Sergei Mikhailovich (1898–1948), Russian film director.

Fox, George (1624–91), founder of Society of Friends (Quakers).

Grierson, John (1898–1972), documentary film-maker.

Hare, William (1790–*c*. 1860), Irish murderer; with William Burke supplied bodies for dissection.

Hassan ibn al-Sabbah (fl. 1090), founder of sect known as Assassins.

Horne, Janet (d. 1727), last woman executed as a witch in Scotland.

Hunter, John (1728–93), physiologist and surgeon.

Hunter, William (1718–83), anatomist and obstetrician.

Jenner, Edward (1749–1823), physician; pioneered vaccination.

Kentigern, Saint (*c*. 518–603), patron saint of Glasgow, also known as Mungo; born Culross.

Kossuth, Louis (1802–94), Hungarian patriot and national leader.

Lunardi, Vincent (1759–1806), early balloonist.

Macfarlan, James (1832–62), poet and pedlar.

Merlin, semi-legendary 6th-century northern British bard.

Muir, John (1838–1914), naturalist and pioneer conservationist.

Omar Khayyam (*c*. 1048–1122), Persian poet and mathematician.

Pelagius (*c*. 355– *c*. 425), British theologian.

Roderick or Rhydderch, 6th-century king of Strathclyde.

Sappho (fl. 600 BC), Greek lyric poet.

Smith, Adam (1723–90), economist, Professor of Moral Philosophy at Glasgow University.

Smith, Madeleine (1835–1928), daughter of Glasgow architect; tried in 1857 for poisoning her lover; verdict Not Proven.

Souter, Brian (b. 1954), transport operator; opposed repeal of Section 28.

Tennant, John (1796–1878), chemist and industrialist.

Thennoch (6th century), mother of Kentigern, Glasgow's patron saint; her name survives in garbled form in St Enoch's Square, Glasgow.

Trocchi, Alexander (1925–84), poet and novelist.

Turing, Alan (1912–54), mathematician; prosecuted for homosexuality, committed suicide.

Watt, James (1736–1819), engineer and inventor.

Whitman, Walt (1819–92), American poet.

Winning, Cardinal Thomas (1925–2001), Archbishop of Glasgow.